KWEZI™

COLLECTOR'S EDITION
ISSUE: 4-6

KWEZI IS A PRODUCT OF
© LOYISOMKIZEART (PTY) LTD (2016)

COLLECTOR'S EDITION (ISSUES 4-6)
PUBLISHED 2016 BY DAVID PHILIP PUBLISHERS
6 SPIN STREET
CAPE TOWN
8001
SOUTH AFRICA

ISBN: 978-1-4856-2297-0
E PUB ISBN: 978-1-4856-2204-8

COVER DESIGN BY: LOYISO MKIZE
ILLUSTRATION: LOYISO MKIZE
COLOURING: CLYDE BEECH
INKING: MBUYISELO MANKAYI AND LOYISO MKIZE
POST PRODUCTION: LOYISO MKIZE AND CLYDE BEECH
STORY: LOYISO MKIZE AND CLYDE BEECH

PRINTED BY Novus Print Solutions

DAVID PHILIP IS COMMITTED TO A SUSTAINABLE FUTURE
FOR OUR BUSINESS, OUR READERS AND OUR COUNTRY.

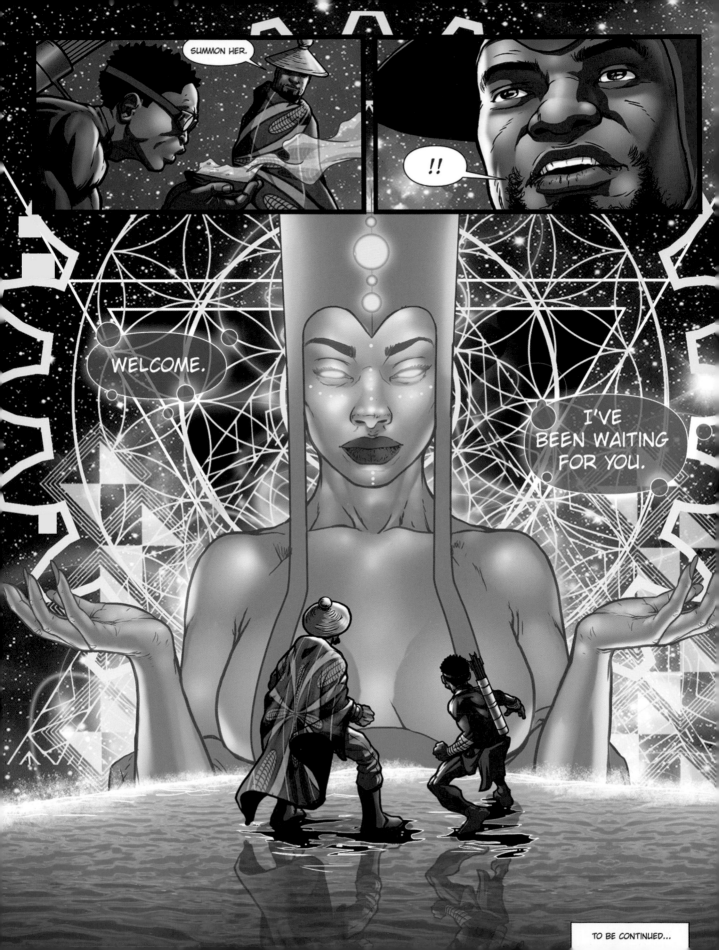

TO BE CONTINUED...

I CAN HEAR YOU.

I SEE YOU NOW. I SEE YOU FOR WHAT YOU REALLY ARE.

IT CAN'T BE.

BU... WAIT, I...

YOU'VE BEEN PLAYING ME THROUGH MY DOUBTS AND FEARS...

BUT NOW, YOU NO LONGER HAVE CONTROL OVER ME.

TO BE CONTINUED...

TEAM KWEZI

Loyiso Mkize was born in Butterworth and is now based in Cape Town. He is the founder of Loyiso Mkize Art and creator of Kwezi comics. As a visual artist, he has specialised both in Illustration and the fine arts. He has been in the comic book scene for nearly ten years and has been involved in numerous South African comic books. His fine arts career spans seven years with four solo exhibitions and six group exhibitions with a keen following both locally and internationally. He enjoys painting, reading comics and other books as well as engaging talks. He hopes his work will leave a lasting contribution to his industry, internationally.

Clyde Beech was born and bred in Cape Town. Even though things didn't quite work out for him in the beginning, once he got his foot in the door as a professional artist he managed to turn it into a career. At present he specialises as a comic book colorist, digital painter and art director. He has also had a stint in 2D animation as a background and texture artist. Being a geek, he loves comics, gaming and pop culture but that comes with a twist, he's also an avid martial artist. As a professional, his goal is to build a viable comic book industry for future artist in this country.